A BLACK MAN IS:

A LOVE LIKE NO OTHER

by

Lee Swann of Baltimore,

MD, USA

My Black Man born from a
black woman
To a world where he's guilty
before proven innocent
Weight on his shoulders before
he can balance
His circumstances as he ages, he
will have to circumvent

My Black Man raised in areas
he will see become gentrified
Educated in schools without the
tools, the access, or the drive
To speak well to their growing
black boys by telling them it is

okay to look a white man in his
eyes to say "I should not have to
be afraid of being alive"

My Black Man enters the world
always poised never uncouth
Facing discrimination not just
for the color of his skin
Other issues too, Being looked
down upon, worked against
The level of scrutiny for just
taking an exhale out, an inhale
in

Stereotypes speak loudly to a
false character less than grand
So unfair he is not permitted to
paint it, his own mural
He has to be strong enough to
take a stand
But will he be allowed
I ponder as he leaves will this be
the last I see of him
Hard to show but my heart's
pain would be indescribable
While presented impenetrable if
anything were to happen
I don't think the soul within my
body would be revivable

Wandering aimlessly I would
walk the roads he once traveled
I would eat the foods he once
loved out of remembrance
Things would just never be the
same without him
And this is how I feel about all
of them

Black Men have been torn down
throughout history
Black Men have been beaten
Black Men have had their rights
revoked truthfully
I believe Black Men deserve
much better treatment

Instead of assuming the worst,
ignore that Helen of Troy
Though beautiful and enticing,
she is just a decoy
Designed and strategically
placed to lure you to the evil
ploy
To make you think a Black
Man's purpose is to destroy

This is utter nonsense
You need to re-examine the
manual in which you found that

It is not the physical appearance
more so than the contents
If you really understood those
statements you'd remove them

We cannot let our Black Men
lose their light
Their demons beyond words
what a plight
An experience you don't want
to see first hand
An encounter like no other, a
force to withstand

He comes home Blood trickles
from open wounds
You try to help close them But
there is just too much
With his own thoughts he is
becoming consumed

Sweat leaves a glaze on his
forehead
You are there with a towel to
soak some of it up
But the perspiration just keeps
pouring instead
It rushes more than the towel
can suck it up

You have to, he has to go back
out there
But you know no one else cares
this intensely
No one would stop for him,
probably just stare
Keep walking past him on the
street stepping on his feet
Why is it completely different
treatment you see
All we ever wanted as a people
was equality
Yet it's been a constant struggle
Both in the light & undercover

Because you know there are
people still oblivious to
The actions they see on the
news they don't find insidious

Staying in their small enclosed
little bubble
I bet I could make that bubble
pop
So rather than relying on others
to build up my Black Men
I want to bring that world of
dissent to a full stop

If the world will not
acknowledge us

If the world will not
acknowledge them
If the world refuses to see past
the shade
If the world refuses to see past
the tone of old men

It is our duty
It is our right
It is our privilege
It is our fight

To bring peace home
To invite the healing in
To reconnect with our nurturing
side

To allow for harmony to be
present
Yes, please, let that set in

If you have a Black Man on
your arm
If you wake up next to that King
every day
I know it's going to be a hard
journey if you don't already
I am taking this trip too We are
going slow and steady

Slow and steady wins the race I
am told

Please do not quit, It will be worth it
In the end to watch that Man grow
Into the Man that will be able to let his everlasting love flow

It will take patience
It will take strength
Do yourself the service of talking through the pain

It will take courage
It will take humility

The end result will be a joy
unimaginable to gain

It will take leniency
It will take strictness
Choose to use each of these
appropriately, it will not be in vain

It will take long days
It will take even longer nights
Sometimes it will overwhelm you,
overload your brain

You are going to need a good
friend, A solid mattress
A well-balanced hobby, Healthy
eating habits

Possibly and almost with full
certainty a competent therapist

Learn now, not later, you must
be able to carry yourself first
Maintain you by yourself for a
time
Lonely it will be, don't worry
you will be fine

On occasion he may forget to
tell you his plans
He might forget to show he
appreciates you how you like
You may end up doing tasks
normally Requiring a man

Do your best to remember it is
not out of spite
Remind yourself his work has to
be the main focus
Remember he has to be a better
him So he can contribute to you
so you all will become us

Curb the urge to yell back when
tones are raised
Do your utmost to be the calm
one in the room
All those bad harmful words,
even if eloquently phrased
Grab the broom Sweep them
away

Remove it from this space
starting today
Be ready to take the weight
It will be heavy
So when they trickle in enjoy
the lighter days

You will be dreaming while
wide awake
Watching his tribulations you
will get weary
You partially believe this will
forever be you all's fate:
Survival mode

Check to check splurging for a
piece of pie
Telling yourself not yet no
vacations to be had
Working overtime more days
than can be quantified
Both hustling strengthening
your team to be ironclad

You realize you cannot work for
anyone else
It may happen at different times
Long game is always a winner
when working on one's self
You start talking about legacy,
feels so good to speak on

Almost like you are committing
a crime to think so freely
Endless ideas of what could be
coming through clearly

Every night as you come
together to rest
You lay with him as he sleeps
right on his chest
You listen to his heartbeat as
you press your ear right to it
You try to match his breaths;
you try to match his beat

As you lay, You stroke his
beard ever so softly

Wishing him only sweet
thoughts and clarity
You would hate for his sleep to
be another test
He deserves to at least have a
good night's rest

Naturally, he was sprawled out
without a blanket
You cuddle closer to him, your
legs intertwine
You pull the covers over you
both
You whisper I love that you are
all mine

These sweet nothings don't
present as needed
If you told him, you sleep on his
heart because you hope to learn
to love as he does
If you told him, you think about
him all day just because
If you told him, you admire the
way he controls conversations
You wish to match his energy
his powerful vibrations
You want to protect him in the
same way he protects you
Rise above the negativity and
the pessimism as it protrudes
From the ugly world around you

Beat the odds and allow success
to settle
Yes, it's possible he probably
wouldn't believe you

He would think you are an
imposter
Who has inhabited you all of a
sudden
Who is this woman in whom
these traits have fostered
Where has this type of love
been

Was it here the duration

It's scary when you finally get
something you ask for
Yet it's this satisfying sensation
To feel like you finally
unlocked the door

Behind this door were all these
requests piled up
A backed-up mail room to
which you now have the key
Open up and read the
unanswered letters
Delivered to you but you could
not pick them up
Neither of you were ready

That was before
We are on the come up
We are on the prowl
Taking whatever is set in our
sights
To take what belongs to you
To take back what is your life

I plead you build up the Black
Man
He stuck with you through his
hardship and your own
He endured your attitude and
your harsh tones

When it mattered, he showed
you love you've never known

It will be worth it I promise
Get rid of the natural impulse to
argue
The instinct reaction to defend
Upon you he is reliant to keep
him far from the deep end

We have to find our words
Black Women, our words are
beyond inspiring
They enlighten the uninformed

They beam lost ones up to new
heights

Nations are birthed on our backs
Other women's children fed
from our breasts
Medicines stolen from our
blood
Solutions made up in our DNA
Yet we are treated as none of
this means anything
You know who it means
something to

That Black Man you spoiled and
treated like a King

The One you upheld at his
weakest points
That Black Man you massaged
when he felt pain in his joints

The One for whom you chose to
be present for
That Black Man you told you
would stand for and adore
The One you would love like no
one before or after
And promised to have a whole
book not just a chapter
Your lives will be greater than
the preceding

Your futures will be more
happiness than grieving
Leave your old thoughts behind
Embrace the new within your
mind

Allow it to flow to your heart,
Create a genesis of your own
Do not delay in pressing start,
Hit reset, get in your zone

Change your patterns
Adopt new routines
Update your vocabulary
Only specific language used in
your messages from now on

For it is by the words you say to
yourself
And the will of your soul that
you keep yourself from being
anyone's pawn

Empower Him
Push Him
Lead when it's your turn
Yes, you will get a turn

Tell him everything you need
him to be he is
It's a psychologic game,
childish in some way maybe
You hear it and it sounds lame

But a life without real and pure
love is one in the same
A life without support and
strength to be shared amongst a
partner who shares your harsh
realities
You run the risk of going insane

No one ever said it wouldn't
work though
The more you say something
aloud the more it flows
So let's try something different
No longer will we allow our
homes to be filled with division

My Black Man Has Vision, He is a Visionary
My Black Man is Powerful, Any Load He Can Carry

My Black Man Withstands Any Derision
My Black Man Controls His Emotions as He Makes Decisions
My Black Man is Gentle, A Quality You Can't Fathom to Possess
My Black Man is Not Dangerous, He is Kind

My Black Man is The Reason
Why I Can Rest
Because My Black Man is My
Protector, He is My Best Friend
My Black Man Will Know I
Have His Back Until the End

He'll be Full of Love, Allowed
to Embrace and Display his
Soul
My Black Man I wish to get
older with you, that is the goal

My Black Man You are
Everything You are Supposed to
Be

When Others Fail You, You
Can Look to Me
I Am Your Black Woman
I shall have no other lover
I shall have no true secret
keeper, you are like no other

When you see someone else
doing better know you will get
there too
While we walk through the fire,
Squeeze the handle tight doing
best to extinguish
But remember even with the
fires out, hold dear this job to

consistently love of a Real
Black Man
As it is never finished

Dedicated to All My Black Men

Around the World

Most Importantly to My One

You Know Who You Are…

www.ingramcontent.com/pod-product-compliance
Lightning Source LLC
Chambersburg PA
CBHW040930110726
48006CB00001B/140